YOUNG
FUNNY
AND

A STAND-UP COMEDY GUIDE
FOR TEENS

**DAVID
SMITHYMAN**

CONCEIVED BY
JO ANN GROSSMAN AND KAREN BERGREEN

ISBN: 1478161752

ISBN-13: 978-1478161752

Thanks to Darlene Violette, Jane Condon, Emma Gonzalez and Mickey Guagno for helping us form this program. To Chris Mazzilli and the Gotham Comedy Club staff, with special mention to Brad Sampey. Thanks to Stu Morden, co-founder of Kids 'N Comedy, for his humor, love of teaching and his editorial steering. Thanks to Ryan Fishman for his cover design and his help with this project, and last but not least, to all of the kids who have inspired us with their creative, original material.

If we have left anyone out, send an email and we'll let you play us in the big budget movie adaptation of the book (if we can't get anybody more famous or good-looking).

- The Kids 'N Comedy Team

YOUNG, FUNNY AND UNBALANCED

CONTENTS

YOUNG, FUNNY AND UNBALANCED

WHO IS THIS BOOK FOR?

So, you have our little book in your hands. How you got it, nobody knows. Maybe you found it in a pile of books in your library. Maybe a cool friend or relative gave it to you for your birthday. Maybe a bird stole it from some other lucky kid who legitimately owned it and dropped it directly into your hands. However it happened, we're happy you found us. And now that you have it, let's get to business. What is this book about, and is it right for me? Good question. Let's find out.

To help you work out whether or not this book is for you, we've compiled a handy checklist. All you have to do is to read through it and check off the things that apply to you. Do us a favor and fill it in pencil, k? Because you never know when a bird might pick up your book off your dresser, and drop it off in the hands of some other lucky kid who wants to fill out this checklist for himself. Cool. Ready? Then, let's begin:

Do you have a brain?

Does it work?

Are you...smart?

Are you cool?

Are you so cool that sometimes other kids don't realize how cool you are?

Are you so cool that sometimes YOU don't even realize how cool you are?

Do you have something to say?

Phew. That was hard. I'm glad it's over. Let's see how you did. If you answered 'Yes' to any of the above questions, then this book is probably right for you. If you didn't, well...you're currently living minus a brain, so chances are you are probably eating this book as we speak. For the rest of you, let's get down to business.

This is a book about writing and performing stand-up comedy. Not the history of stand-up comedy, or the kind of clothes stand-up comics wear, or how a microphone is able to make our voices louder. Nope. This book is about writing and performing YOUR OWN stand-up comedy routine. Amazing, right? We think so too. And we're not going to pretend it's a cinch, because let's face it, nothing worth doing has ever been super easy to do. That's just how life works. Take any amazing human feat throughout history and you'll find that whoever performed it spent a lot of time getting it wrong before finally getting it right.

Take Ben Franklin, for example. Do you think he discovered electricity on his first try? No way! Do you think it was easy? Not a chance. That guy had to stand outside in a thunder storm and fly a kite around. Alone. Can you even imagine how stupid that must have looked to everybody who walked by? People probably shouted all kinds of mean things at Ben Franklin. Things like: "Having fun, Ben?" or "Ever heard of an umbrella, Ben?" (Okay, I didn't say they were shouting particularly clever mean things at him. But, let's face it; nobody who shouts mean things at other people ever has anything particularly clever to say.) The point is, he risked looking stupid a couple of times, until he eventually discovered electricity, and now everybody remembers him for being awesome. The same goes for learning to do stand-up comedy. Maybe the first joke you write doesn't make anybody laugh. Who cares? Write another one. And another one. And another one. And if you keep writing jokes, eventually you'll write one that makes somebody who overhears you chuckle. Or maybe even squirt milk out their nose. Such is the power of stand-up comedy.

This book is for young people with a good sense of humor and something to say. You don't have to be the funniest person in your class, or your school, or even your family (although it wouldn't hurt). You don't have to be the best looking, or the coolest. In fact, people who think of themselves as being really cool and good-looking are often gigantic jerks. Like, zero fun to be around. Cool, good-looking people don't make jokes, they don't get jokes, they don't even say anything interesting! They just look at themselves in the mirror all day, and brag about how many people have told them that they should be a model. So this book is not concerned with them. This book is for young people with substance.

And don't get me wrong, having substance doesn't mean that you're ugly and you smell bad. I mean, statistically, some of you probably do, but that's not your fault. Puberty makes everybody gross for a while. Nothing you can do about it. The point is that smelling bad or not, a person of substance is a person who has something important to say. Somebody who uses their brain, who thinks critically, who notices when something is weird or strange, who has an active imagination, who has big ideas. Somebody who is okay being exactly who they are, regardless of how many times people have told them they should or shouldn't be a model.

This book can't teach you to be funny. If you don't have a good imagination, this book can't give you one. This book can't make you popular, or get you a girlfriend or a boyfriend, or make your parents let you borrow their car to go see a movie on a school night. It can't buy you a donut, or knit you a warm sweater, or take your dog for a walk when it's raining outside. Really, this book is only good for one thing: pushing you. That's it. It'll give you tips, and handy hints, and helpful exercises, and encouragement, but when it comes down to actually writing funny things that will make other people laugh? All on you, dude.

That said, if you've read this far without throwing this book through a window, or into a swimming pool, you've already taken a huge step on the way to being the funniest, smartest, non-jerkiest stand-up comedian you can be. We might not be able to travel all the way out to your living room and write jokes with you, but we can hopefully give you the tools you need to start writing (and even performing) stand-up comedy on your own. So, without further ado, finish that grilled cheese you're munching on, wipe your hands on your t-shirt, and let's turn the page and get started.

- The Kids 'N Comedy Team

Chapter 1

WHERE DO I FIND MATERIAL?

Good question. This is probably one of the toughest parts of being a stand-up comedian, so it's probably smart that we get it out of the way first. Are you ready for the answer? It's going to change your life. Ready? Are you sure? Okay, then. You asked for it. The answer is...

...everywhere.

Okay, that was sneaky. I apologize. But it's also totally true. I wish there was a special material drawer that I could tell you to open whenever you needed something funny to say, but unfortunately for everybody involved, it just doesn't exist. Instead, you sort of have to start opening up drawers all over the place, and hope that you stumble upon something awesome that you can use in your stand-up act. And you will. If you look hard enough. (And of course, I'm using drawers as a metaphor here. I don't want to get any letters from angry Moms and Dads complaining to me that their son or daughter has been opening up drawers all over the house looking for jokes, and now there are socks and underwear all over the floor).

I'm a firm believer that you can write stand-up about pretty much anything. And I mean anything. It doesn't matter what it is. As long as you think it's worth saying into a microphone, I think it's worth an audience listening to - as long as you do it right. And how do you do it right? <u>You care about it</u>. You've got to think it's important, otherwise what's the point? If you don't care about cats, don't write material about cats. Because you're going to get bored doing it, and as soon as you get bored, the audience is going to get bored, and when people get bored, they start checking their cell phones, and thinking about their dishes, and their shopping lists, and that big meeting at work on Monday, and they stop listening to you. So, if you want people to listen, write about stuff that counts.

Stuff that's important to you. Stuff that, you know, matters. And maybe that is cats. I don't know. It could be napkins for all I know. Or jigsaw puzzles. Or old people smelling like the insides of a suitcase (they do, sometimes.) It doesn't have to matter to me. I'm not important. In stand-up, the most important person is Y-O-U. Sounds selfish, but it's true. That doesn't mean that everything you say is perfect. Don't get me wrong. You still have to care about your audience, and make things relatable to them. Just don't pander to them. Write for you first. Then them. If you genuinely care about what you're saying, so will they.

Okay, so now you're probably thinking: "I'm important. Got it. And I should write about what matters to me? Okay. But what if I don't know what matters to me yet? I'm young. I have years to figure that stuff out. Stop pressuring me to grow up. Stop telling me what to do. Get off my back. You're not my real Dad." And you would be right. I'm not. And that's good for both of us, trust me. I would forget you inside of a Walmart before you could say 'irresponsible parent.' Anyway, your question is still a good one. That being: how do I work out what matters and what doesn't? Well, I can't really help you with that. I could tell you what matters to me, but that wouldn't really help you, would it? So, it might sound like a cop-out, but you sort of just have to work it out. And you will, if you spend like 5 minutes thinking about it. To get you started, I say we make a list. Do me a favor, and try not to over think it.

PUTTING THE U IN STAND UP COMEDY

1. I spend a lot of time thinking about _____

2. I know a whole butt-load about _____

3. Nothing annoys me more than _____

4. The coolest fact I know is _____

5. If I could change one thing about myself it would be

_____

6. I am deathly afraid of _____

Okay, how'd you do? Probably pretty well considering you didn't have to study at all. Or read anything. If only school were so easy! And now you know 5 new things about yourself, all of which are great starting points for writing your awesome, kick-ass stand-up routine. Way to go, you. Now, let's go through your answers.

1. I spend a lot of time thinking about _____

This one's important because if you think about something a lot, it probably means it's important to you. If when you're in school and you find yourself daydreaming about what it would be like to be a bird, or what kind of father you would be, or what the future would be like, or how astronauts go to the bathroom, then that's something worth considering putting into your routine. Chances are, if you're thinking about it, somewhere somebody is probably thinking about it too. (How DO astronauts go to the bathroom??? Somebody tell me!)

2. I know a whole butt-load about _____

Everybody knows a whole butt-load about something. For me, that something is animals. I love animals. They're so awesome. And pretty amazing, too. Did you know bees communicate through dance? That never stops being fascinating to me. Although I am extremely happy that we humans get to talk to each other, otherwise I would only be able to communicate one thing: "I'm a terrible dancer." So, whatever it is that you know lots about, that's a good place to look for potential stand-up material. Not only do you probably know some stuff that we don't, but if you're going to get up on stage and talk about something to a room full of people, you should probably know what you're talking about. You ever have that experience where you forget to do a book report, and instead of telling your teacher that you didn't read the book, you just sort of wing it? Remember how successful that normally is? "Um. So, it's about these kids that live in Terebithia, and they, like, um...love this bridge or whatever...yeah." Well, that's what it would sound like if you were to do stand-up about something you didn't know anything about. So, do yourself a favor and write about stuff you DO know about. It's way easier.

3. Nothing annoys me more than _____

OMG, can you believe that thing? Ugh. Isn't that thing like the absolute worst? I mean, seriously. I can't even believe that thing is allowed to exist, that's how much it annoys me. Am I right? AM I???

Of course I am. Because we all get annoyed by stuff. It's human nature. And, in stand-up, what you hate is always infinitely funnier and more interesting than what makes you happy. I know that sounds weird, but it's true. Think about it: would you want to hear somebody who just bought an Xbox talk about how amazing their Xbox is? Absolutely not. That's boring. Nobody ever wants to hear that.

But somebody who wanted an Xbox and got a Wii? Now, that's funny.

4. The coolest fact that I know is _____

Facts are seriously underrated. I blame high school. Always trying to make everybody memorize facts that they don't want to, and probably will never need to remember. But for every boring fact about what year somebody elected somebody else to something-or-other, there's like ten awesome facts that stay with you forever. Like, for instance, did you know during the 19th century in England, dentists ran out of human teeth?! That's crazy. What's crazier is that people's teeth still fell out all the time, so you know what they did? They used animal teeth. ANIMAL TEETH. Can you imagine? People wandering around smiling with dog's teeth and pig's teeth in their mouths? That's cray-cray. Anyway, the point is that stand-up, when it's really good, can not only amuse you, it can teach you something you didn't know before. And that's your job. Do that for an audience. Talk to them about something that's super interesting AND super hilarious. Luckily, you have, like 5000 years of recorded human history to sift through.

5. If I could change one thing about myself it would be

_____

Nobody is perfect. Especially stand-up comics. We're probably the least perfect of anybody. But that's good for us. Or good for our stand-up, anyway. Because nobody likes hearing about cool, perfect people being really cool and perfect. In fact, there's nothing more boring. Let's look at this joke as an example.

"I'm terrified of walking through bad neighborhoods. It's not that I think everybody's going to mug me...it's that I know everybody could."

Not the best joke ever, I'll admit. But we're under pressure here, so give me a break. The reason it works is because it sounds like the joke is going to come at the expense of the people living in the bad neighborhood, but then, instead, the joke comes at the expense of the person telling it. Basically, the point being made is: I'm not prejudiced, I'm just a huge wuss. Which is funny. Because you know else is a huge wuss? Most people. Some of us are just better at hiding it than others. Now let's re-write that joke from the perspective of somebody perfect.

"I'm not terrified of walking through bad neighborhoods. Why would I be? I'm awesome." Yep. The worst. Anyway, work out what's wrong with you and write jokes about it. It'll almost always work.

6. I am deathly afraid of _____

Hey, you know what's terrifying? Everything. Seriously, though. Things are terrifying when you think about them. Germs are on everything all the time. Spiders crawl into our mouths when we fall asleep. Manhole covers explode and kill like 8 people a year. The list goes on and on. The point is, everybody's scared of something. Some of us, like yours truly, are scared of all kinds of things. And you know what makes people feel better about being scared of stuff? Hearing other people be scared of stuff too. It's infinitely interesting. And the weirder your fear is, the more we care about listening you talk about it. Because your crippling fear of colorful birds makes us feel way less weird about our own fear of spiders, and snakes, and sharks, and all those other things that normal people are scared of. So, do me a favor and work out what scares you. Then try making fun of yourself about it. The jokes practically write themselves.

Okay, now that that's over and done with, you should have a list of at least six (and in reality, probably way more!) things for you to write stand-up comedy about. Also, because you've been answering these questions honestly and truthfully, your stand-up will be as original and unique as you are. Nice going, you. Also, because it's true, you'll actually care about it. And it will pretty much write itself. There won't be any sitting at your desk, scratching your head with a pencil and racking your brain to come up with things to make fun of. Just some good ol' fashioned introspection. And because you're dipping into that limitless expanse of comedy gems that is your adolescent brain, you'll never run out of material!*

*Unless your brain falls out, or you contract brain worms, or you get hit in the head with football and forget who you are. If any of that happens, disregard everything I've said. You're totally on your own.

Chapter 2

HOW DO I TURN MY IDEAS INTO STAND-UP IDEAS?

Another good question. You're full of those. Now, this one doesn't have a trick answer, because it's a tricky enough problem already, without me trying to confuse you. This is easily probably the hardest part of stand-up. No question. Because you can't really teach somebody how to do it. I know that sounds like a funny thing to read in a how-to-do book, but that isn't really what this book is about. It's more of a companion. Like a helpful comedy gnome. It can't write jokes for you, but it can hand you sharpened pencils when you need them, or fetch you a glass of milk and maybe a chocolate chip cookie if you're stuck on a particularly tricky joke. This book is here to help you, but it only works as hard as you do. So, with that said, let's try and turn some of those things you came up with in chapter 1 into jokes.

Step One: Come up with a premise

BIG RULE: It's not enough to just say something is weird, or stupid, or crazy. Even if it is all of those things. Because thinking something is weird, or stupid, or crazy is only the first step on the way to writing your joke. You're not doing anything we can't do on our own. Oh, the fact that koalas have fingerprints is weird? Yeah, guess what. We know. So what? What are you going to do about it?

This is where your premise comes in. Think of your premise as the glue that holds your bit together. It's the central, underlying idea behind what you're saying. It's your thesis statement. It's your WHY.

It's your WHAT IF. It's the idea that you had that nobody else did. So how do we come up with one? I'll tell you. We begin to Unpack.

Wait, you're thinking, "unpack?" Like a suitcase? That's exactly what I'm saying. Zip open that weird thing you noticed, and start taking everything out. Only instead of taking out pairs of underwear and tennis shoes, you take out facts and ideas and observations and concerns, and anything you can think of that relates to that idea. Google it and see what comes out. Go to the library and get out some books on it. Just gather information, and as much as you can. And keep doing it until you find something that makes your brain light up in that way that only good ideas can. You'll never know when it's going to happen, but trust me, when it does, it's worth it.

PREMISE EXAMPLE #1

Let's try using this koala fingerprints idea as an example. We learned in chapter 1 that sometimes the world around us can offer us some amazing stand-up material. I recently read in one of those Amazing Facts for Kids books they sell in bookstores that koalas have fingerprints. Which I thought was pretty amazing. So I went home and Googled it, and guess what I found out? Like a million interesting things about koalas having fingerprints. And I knew there was something in there that I could write a bit about. I could feel it. I just didn't know what yet. Until I read this:

"Koalas fingerprints and human fingerprints are so similar that the two are virtually indistinguishable."

And my brain lit up. Because not only is that amazing, it's practically begging for somebody to write a joke about it. So I began to unpack it, taking out every idea I could think of that related to it. Like so:

- Koalas are adorable.

- They have fingerprints (which is amazing.)

- We have fingerprints (which is less amazing.)

- Our fingerprints look the same as theirs (even more amazing.)

- Why are fingerprints important? Hmmm. Ooh! I got it! Crime scenes!

- So, if a koala committed a crime, it would leave fingerprints that looked like our fingerprints! (now we're cooking!)

- So, you could commit a crime USING a koala and totally get away with it! (even better!)

- Or if somebody found your fingerprints at a crime scene, you could totally be like "It wasn't me. It was a koala."

- Or if you ever wanted to commit a crime, you should totally do it in a koala enclosure. That place would be full of fingerprints!

See, now we're getting somewhere. Not only have we established the perfect way to commit petty crimes, but we've also come up with some potentially hilarious situations. It's not perfect yet, but we're on our way. Eventually, we could probably write a pretty great joke about how always carrying around a koala provides the perfect criminal defense for almost anything.

Something like:

So, koalas have fingerprints. Not only that, but their fingerprints are so similar to ours, that they'd be almost indistinguishable at a crime scene. Not only is that amazing, but I also totally plan on using it as my defense if I'm ever put on trial for murder.

They'd be like:

"Mr. Smithyman, how do you explain your fingerprints being all over the scene of the crime?"

and I'd be like:

"My fingerprints, counselor? <u>Or those of a koala with a score to settle</u>?"

Not perfect yet, but we're on our way. And that's how jokes work. They're almost never perfect the first time. Or even the one-hundredth time. That's why you gotta keep working at them. But at the very least we have an idea that nobody else had (as far as we know), and that's a pretty damn good start.

PREMISE EXAMPLE #2

Let's try another one. One of the teenagers, David Thompson, in our shows was out one day when he noticed a grown man sitting outside at a cafe, eating lunch, opposite a golden retriever. The golden retriever was sitting on a seat, just watching the guy eat. Pretty weird, right? Now there's probably a perfectly reasonable explanation for this, but if there is, we don't care what it is. Because reasonable explanations aren't funny. We want the story behind the story. We want the weirdest, funniest reason those two are hanging out having lunch. So, we come up with a premise. And how do we do that? We begin unpacking the idea. Like so:

- Why would a guy have lunch with a dog?

- Was the dog happy about it?

- Why wasn't the guy having lunch with another human being?

- Is he lonely?

- What would the dog order?

- What would they talk about?

- It would probably be really awkward.

- Like a really terrible...first date!

And our brains light up again. Because there's our premise. Guy on a first date with a dog. That's awesome. Great premise. And that's exactly what Thompson did with it. Here's his joke:

So, the other day I saw this guy having lunch at a cafe opposite a dog. Like the dog was sitting on a seat. And they were both just sitting there in silence, not eating. It was really weird. And I was like, this guy is either a really considerate dog owner...or this is the worst blind date of all time.

That's a great joke. Because you can totally picture it. Which is really important for a good joke. It should paint a funny picture in our minds. Imagine Thompson's premise: this guy going on a blind date, making lunch reservations, only to show up and find out that his date is a real dog...literally. Thompson goes on to make a bunch of jokes off of that premise, about what the dog's dating profile might have said, what their conversation would be like, etc. etc. etc. The point is: a solid premise is integral to writing solid jokes. Your premise is your joke's skeleton, remember? Without a solid skeleton, things get real messy. Imagine your own body with a crappy skeleton. All your organs would be falling out all over the place, and people would be tripping over them. Bleugh. Gross. No, thank you. So, keep them tight and solid. It will serve you in the long run.

Now, that I've given you a couple of examples, let's give you a chance to write some premises of your own. Remember the steps:

1. Notice/read/learn/realize something (about yourself or the world around you)

2. Is it weird/interesting/strange/bizarre/stupid/sad/crazy?

3. If so, why? Use your imagination.

4. Start unpacking that baby and writing down everything that comes out.

5. Keep doing that until you find that idea that makes your brain light up like a light bulb.

6. Write down that idea. That's your premise.

Okay, your turn. Turn the page and get started. Good luck!

MY FIRST PREMISE

I noticed/read/learned/realized that

_____

_____

This is weird/interesting/strange/bizarre/stupid/sad/crazy because

_____

_____

UNPACKING LIST:

-   -

-   -

-   -

-   -

-   -

-   -

-   -

AHA! MY BRAIN LIT UP! HERE'S MY NEW PREMISE:

_____

_____

Brain Worms Exercise

Note: You'll find these Brain Worm exercises scattered throughout the book. I called them Brain Worms because I hope that they'll burrow their way into your frontal lobe, and help you write jokes. Fill them in as you go!

1. Impressions

Can you do any impressions? Only one way to find out. Start mimicking people you see on television, or people you know, or your friend's parents, or pretty much anybody. It'll train you to pay attention to people's quirks, and recognize how to use them to comedic effect. You never know who you can do an impression of you until you try doing it. Also, even if you don't end up using your impressions in your stand-up, it's always a hit at parties.

Chapter 3

WRITING JOKES

Okay, this chapter's going to be even harder to explain than the last one (if that's possible). Because this one is about doing something that I definitely can't teach you to do. And that's: be funny. Hopefully for both of us, you are already a little funny. Or a lot funny. That would be even better. But don't be discouraged if you're only a little funny - practice makes perfect. It's true for tennis, it's true for origami, and it's true for stand-up comedy. Sure, if all your jokes make people want to throw themselves off of bridges, then you're probably never going to be sidesplittingly hilarious. But you might improve. And if you work hard at it, and pay attention to which jokes work and which don't, then maybe, after a while, the people you tell them to might only jump off of their bunk bed, or diving boards, instead of off a bridge to their untimely demise. Okay, now that we're clear on that, let's take the next step:

HOW DO I WRITE JOKES?

So, it's tricky. And I feel silly telling you that there is any single way to do it, because let's face it, there isn't. And anybody who tells you that there is, is just trying to save themselves some work. I can tell you how I write jokes, but who's to say that that would work for you? It's like asking somebody what's the best way to eat a hamburger? Do you take off the tomato and the onions? Or do you ask for extra? Do you start by eating the french fries? Or do you leave them till the end? The possibilities are endless. The truth is there's no one right way to write a joke. You just have to sort of figure out what works for YOU. That said, there are a couple of techniques that I use to try and think of funny things, and I'm going to share them with you. I'm by no means an expert, but I do spend my Saturday's at Kids 'N Comedy teaching kids to write jokes, so hopefully I can at least offer you some handy hints. Before we begin, two things to remember as you write your jokes:

1. Make sure you have a solid premise

First things first: let's dust off that premise you worked on in the last chapter. The premise is the skeleton of your bit, remember? So, that's where all your jokes are going to come from. Also, if you write from your premise, it will help you stay on topic. If your premise is about your mother being overprotective, don't start making jokes about how smelly taxi drivers are (especially considering that so many of them actually smell nice!) So, the premise is going to help you with that.

2. Stay on point

The point can be about anything, but you need to keep making it. Think about your bit as an argument, and your jokes as the best way of illustrating your argument. In the case of David Thompson's bit about the guy eating lunch with the dog, each of the jokes he tells will be convincing you that the two of them are actually on a terrible first date. By the end of the bit, he will have explored that idea so thoroughly that you might even forget that there was any other explanation to why a man might be sitting across from his dog.

Just remember that as soon as you stop building an argument, then we stop understanding why you're talking to us. So, if your premise is about how catching the subway is terrible, use every joke to help build that argument. Write a joke about how smelly it is, write a joke about how dirty it is, write a joke about how it takes forever to get anywhere, but don't, whatever you do, write a joke about how they're doing the best they can, and we should be grateful for all of their hard work. Because that will just confuse us. "I thought he hated the subway?" people will say. Instead, just keep building your argument, and stay on point. By the end of your bit, we should have come around to your way of thinking. And even if we don't feel the same way about the subway as you do by the end of your bit, at least we'll understand why <u>YOU</u> feel that way.

Okay, got it? Let's try and write some jokes.

As an example, I'm going to use something I recently overheard whilst sitting in a park near my house, working on this chapter. By the way, eavesdropping on other people's conversations is a great way to come up with material. Why? Because people are ridiculous. And they have ridiculous conversations all the time. Like, RIDICULOUS. Try it the next time you're sitting in the cafeteria, or riding the bus, or waiting for the movie to start. Just listen to the conversations around you. Not only will you learn a lot of weird stuff about the people around you, but you'll probably be able to turn some it into material for your stand-up routine.

So, anyway, I'm sitting in the park, and I look over and I see this guy playing the game I-Spy with his daughter, who couldn't have been more than 4 years old. And the thing about I-Spy is: I'm amazing at it, like, better than other humans. So, I decide to listen in on their game, and this is what I hear:

Dad: "Okay, are you ready, Stephanie? I'll go first. I spy with my little eye something beginning with 'B'. Got that? 'B'. Something starting with 'B'."

Stephanie: *thinks for a minute* "Um. Balloon?"

Dad: "What? No. The answer is 'Beautiful flowers.'"

Okay, so this is ridiculous. Poor Stephanie. Trying her best to play one of the famously easiest games of all time with a dad who's clearly used to playing at a professional level, and coming up short every time.

And that's what makes it funny: the juxtaposition (look it up) between how intensely the Dad is playing the game (really high), and the ability level of the person he's playing against (really low). And if you can find something like that; something that doesn't sync up, or make sense, or seems crazy, then you're on your way to discovering the joke hidden inside it.

So, Stephanie's Dad is clearly the butt of the joke here. Stephanie's basically a baby, and her Dad is playing a really tough game of I-Spy with her that she clearly has no chance of winning. So, we can make fun of him without feeling bad. He's acting crazy, and he's totally cheating at I-Spy, so he pretty much deserves what he gets.

So, why is it ridiculous that the answer was "beautiful flowers"? Let's unpack it.

I-Spy is called I-Spy because that's what you do when you play it. You just look at something, and then tell somebody the first letter, and they guess it. My family used to play it all the time on road trips. It's not even particularly fun, it's just a way of passing the time. It's definitely not a game that anybody cares about 'winning.' I didn't even know you could win until I watched Stephanie and her Dad (although if you ask me, they're both losing.) But the point is, you spy something like a hedgehog, and you say "I spy something beginning with the letter H" and then the person looks around, sees a hedgehog, guesses it correctly, and everybody feels slightly less bad about being stuck in a car for 8 hours. So, you're supposed to make it sort of obvious for the other person. Here's what's ridiculous about what Stephanie's Dad did:

1. He's playing to win a game that nobody really cares about winning.

2. He's playing that way against a baby.

3. It's his baby.

4. He used an adjective to make it impossibly hard to guess.

All these things are pointing at Stephanie's Dad being a bit overly competitive here. And a bit unrealistic in his expectations for his daughter. So, that sounds like it's going to be our premise:

Premise: This guy is so desperate to win a game of I-Spy that he will play dirty to ensure that his 4 year-old daughter will lose.

Here are some way of mining that premise for jokes:

1. Apply your own logic to situations, and apply your own context.

That's what we initially did to work out why this conversation was ridiculous. We applied our own logic to a seemingly mundane moment in the lives of a man and his daughter, to draw conclusions that they never intended. Basically, we took the elements available to us (the snippet of a game of I-Spy) and worked out a way that it made sense (filled in the blanks.) We did that by coming up for reasons why things were happening. Why did Stephanie's Dad choose "beautiful flowers" as the answer? Because he was desperate to win. Or so we have decided anyway. In reality, it's probably nothing close to that, but that doesn't matter to us. If Stephanie's Dad knew we were writing jokes about him, he might be like: "But that's not what I meant! You know what I meant!" And yes, we do. But that doesn't stop us from being able to pretend we didn't, and totally make fun of him.

Also, the moment that we're making fun of was just a tiny part of a much larger whole. Maybe Stephanie's Dad realized that he was being too hard on her, and eased up on the next round. Maybe he realized his mistake and apologized, and took her for ice-cream. But that isn't funny. So, we're going to pretend that Stephanie's Dad played that way on purpose, and is just a crappy parent. By putting the moment in that context, we can totally rip the situation apart.

In noticing things, feel free to take things you see out of context, and apply your own, in order to write material about them. If you find one shoe in the street, you could probably assume somebody threw it away. But take it out of the context of living in a city where people throw things away. Did somebody lose it? Did it run away?

Maybe a man with one leg buys a pair of shoes and always has to throw one away. <u>You</u> decide! Go nuts!

Applied logic and Context: Stephanie's Dad is cheating to win at I-Spy. He wants so desperately to win, he'll bend the rules to do it.

Joke: "Beautiful flowers"? Um, the game's called I-Spy. Not <u>I-Spy-And-Then-Make-A-Value-Judgment.</u>

2. Stretch it to the limit

Exaggeration is a comic's best friend. Lying is not. And there's <u>definitely</u> a difference. Gone now are the days of "So, I was walking down the street the other day, and _____ happened!" We all know that this didn't happen. Whatever it is. Normally, it's just your way of getting to a punchline that you didn't really earn. There are exceptions to the rule, of course. If you're doing stand-up as a character, or if you do one-liners, the rules of truth are more easily bent. We don't expect character and one-liner comics to necessarily tell us the truth. Their comedy is almost never personally revealing. So, they get a pass.

One of our teenaged comics, Daniel Laitman, is exclusively a one-liner comic. His jokes are meticulously written, and work as tiny little stories, instead of longer, personally-revealing bits.

e.g. "3 out of 4 dentists recommend Crest Toothpaste. I want to know what that fourth dentist knows."

That's Daniel's style, which works for him. And if that style speaks to you, maybe it's your style too. For the rest of us, we're stuck working with the truth.

Wait, you're saying, does that mean I can only tell the exact truth all the time? No. Not by a long shot. But everything you say should come from truth. And that's where exaggeration comes in. A good way to write jokes is to push things to their logical limit. You take things to their extreme. Think of your idea as an elastic band. Your job as the comic is to stretch that idea as far as you possibly can without breaking the elastic.

One of our teenaged comics, Mark Cohen, does a joke about World of Warcraft, the role-playing video game. In the joke, he talks about how his Dad also plays the game, but doesn't understand the point of it. And how instead of going out and fighting orcs and slaying dragons, like he's supposed to do, his Dad just trades items for gold, not interacting with any other players. His punchline to the joke is that in a virtual world where somebody can be anything they want to be, Mark's Dad chooses to be...Mark's Dad. Saving money and being responsible. It's a great joke. And true, too. But the laughs come from Mark's interpretation of the events, and his pushing the idea to its logical limit.

He goes on to say that his Dad is probably amassing all of the virtual gold in order to send Mark to virtual college. We all know that this isn't true, and just an exaggeration, but we get it because it's a logical extension of the original idea: Mark's Dad doesn't understand how to play video games. Once we've bought that premise, Mark can go on to tell us all sorts of crazy, exaggerated examples of what his Dad would be like in video games, and we'll buy it. And we still leave knowing that it all came from a truthful place.

Note: Feel free to use as many people from your real life in your jokes as you want. Just remember to do it with love. There is a difference between making somebody the butt of an excellent joke, and just calling them fat. And don't worry if you can't look or sound like them. Just find the true essence of their character, and then use that to define your characterization of them. Not only will it make it what you're doing real and relatable to an audience, but If you do it right, your target will be laughing the hardest of anybody, and the rest of the audience will be identifying with him. Remember to characterize, not criticize. One comes with love, the other comes with anger.

Exaggeration: Stephanie's Dad picked an answer that was based on his opinion of what was beautiful, not on anything objective. Which is unfair. A game of I-Spy where you had to know the other person intimately to guess the answers would be impossible.

Joke: "I-Spy with my little eye something beginning with 'A.' Yep, it was 'Absent father.' I was spying into my memories!"

3. What If...

This is similar to the last one. Everybody knows what a "what if" scenario is. It's a thought exercise. It's a game for your brain. What if...there were flying cars? What if...cats could talk? What if...whatever. You get the idea. The point is, this is an excellent way of unpacking your idea, and coming up with funny jokes and premises. Let's use Stephanie and her Dad as an example.

We know that Stephanie's Dad plays a mean game of I-Spy. But what if it just got meaner?

What if that weren't the end of the game? What if it only got harder in the next round?

Stephanie's Dad: "Okay, Stephanie. Let's try it again. I-Spy with my little eye something beginning with 'E'. Got that, Stephanie? E.'"

Stephanie: "Ummm...elephant?"

Stephanie's Dad: "Nope! It was the 'Ephemeral nature of time', but nice try. You're getting better."

4. Analogize

Remember those analogies on comprehensive tests? Probably not. But they existed. They would ask you things like:

Cats are to kittens as Dogs are to _____

A: Puppies. (obv.)

Some people hated them, but not me. I thought they were great. And they're good practice for writing jokes, too. An easy way to come up with jokes is to create analogous situations. For example, if you're writing a joke about how bees communicate through dance, (they do that, remember?) you could try applying that idea to a similar situation. Like, how about instead of bees, we replace it with humans. And instead of humans, how about we just say me. I'm a terrible dancer, so I would be terrible at communicating things through dance. And that's sort of a funny idea. So you could probably write a joke like:

Bees communicate through dance. I've been learning how to do that, too. So far, I've mastered the phrases: "I'm a terrible dancer." and "Everybody avoid me."

See how all we did to come up with that was apply the rules of one situation to another one in which it could apply? Good. Let's keep moving.

5. Act Out

This is the simplest one to explain, because it's practically self-explanatory. An act-out is just acting out a punchline for laughs. The conversation we had between Stephanie and her Dad is a perfect example. To deliver that joke, you'd have to play both of them, and have a conversation on stage. You'd have to literally act it out. In an act out, you can get laughs not only from the words you use, but also from the way you stand, the voices you use, the way you move your body, etc. etc. Also, sometimes it's funny to give your characters details the audience wouldn't expect. Maybe Stephanie's Dad is British? Maybe he's German. Nobody can tell you he wasn't, so you get to call the shots. The point is, don't be afraid to illustrate your jokes by adding an act-out or two. Remember: a picture paints a thousand words, and people like seeing other people get a little goofy every now and again. Don't be afraid.

Brain Worms Exercise

Lists - fill in the blanks

Lists are fun. Think of the heading of the list as the setup, and then the items on the list as your punchlines. To help you, I've given you a couple of examples for each.

e.g. "I asked for ice with my soda, but this is ridiculous

Dad jokes made on deck during the sinking of the Titanic !"

"Snow cones, anyone?"

"And I don't even have my bathing suit!"

_____

_____

Poorly-named Butcher shops that went out of business

e.g. Sausage-fest!

Everyone's a wiener!

The Death Emporium!

Failed sequels to popular children's movies

e.g. Aladdin 2: Robin Williams passed.

Mighty Ducks 4: Goldberg's just not getting any better.

Air Bud 5: Covered in Gymnas-ticks!

_____

_____

<u>Band names for a band whose members who secretly hate each other</u>

e.g. Jerks in the Machine

Knife in the Back

Resenta!

_____

_____

Discontinued artisanal Starbucks coffee blends

e.g.   Namibian Toil

Ugandan Hate Crime

Honduran Unrest (Decaf)

_____

_____

Chapter 4

WHAT NOT TO DO

I know, I know, this seems like an overly negative chapter. But it sort of needs to be in here. Because it's easy to make the following mistakes. And if you make them, it won't mean you're a terrible person. And you may even still get laughs. But you won't be reaching your true potential. And that's what I want. And I'm no expert. Let's be clear on that. But I have been helping young people like you do stand-up for a little while now, and I'm starting to notice what works and what doesn't.

Also, let's be clear that I'm not telling you what to do when you grow up and go out into the world on your own. That's all on you. I don't presume to teach adults how to do stand-up. I don't have experience doing that. But teenagers, I get. So I write these rules in the hope that you read them, and think about them. Maybe you'll even follow them. And if you don't, then that's fine too. It won't ruin my day. Because I'm not your Dad. Or your science teacher. Or your guidance counselor. I'm just somebody who made a lot of these mistakes when I was first starting out, and I want you to be better than I was. You guys are the future of stand-up, so sue me if I want you to be clever, and original, and the smartest, funniest young people you can be. Okay, let's get into it before I start crying.

Oh, and one thing before we get into this: a lot of you will read this and say "Wait! My favorite comedian totally breaks these rules!" and to that I will say: there are exceptions to every rule. Especially when it comes to art. But before you go crazy breaking the rules, you should probably learn what they are and why they exist. And when you're rich and famous, feel free to do whatever you want. Cool? Cool.

DON'T...

1. Be racist, homophobic, or misogynistic

This is at number one because it's the most common mistake, and also the least acceptable. At every bad stand-up comedy show in the world there is at least one terrible comedian doing jokes at the expense of people of other races, genders, and sexual orientations. It's honestly the worst. Rape isn't funny. It just isn't. Neither is being homophobic. Or making fun of other races because they're different to you. It's the quickest way to alienate everybody in the room. And every other comedian in the show. It's ignorant, and easy, and nobody respects a comedian who peddles what is easy, and what is ignorant. In my opinion, the point of stand-up comedy is to express yourself in the smartest, most relatable and most honest way possible.

Gay people, women, and people of other races are often the butt of jokes in stand-up comedy. Why? Because they're easy targets. A comedian who picks on gay people for being gay, or women for being women, or Chinese people for being Chinese, is nothing more than a playground bully. And nobody thinks bullies are cool. Except other bullies. Or people who are scared of being bullied themselves. Because bullies are cowards. They pick on kids who are smaller, or weaker than themselves, because they know those kids can't fight back. The same is true of stand-up comedians who make fun of minorities, whichever they might be. Your stand-up comedy should be the purest representation of who you are as a person. When you're writing jokes on your own, always ask yourself: what does this joke say about me? If you're smart, you'll know when you've gone too far.

Note: Does this mean you can't do jokes about anybody that is different from you? Absolutely not. You can. But you have to be clever about it. And it has to come from a place of love. Not hate. You can write a joke about gay people, just as long as the point of the joke isn't to make gay people feel bad. Explore any topic you want. Often the more difficult, the better. Just be sure to do it with love.

2. Make fun of strangers in a hurtful way

This is sort of the same thing as #1. Still, it's worth saying. Your role as a comic should be to endear the audience to you, not to alienate them. Often times at comedy shows, you will see the host picking on people in the audience. Occasionally, this is funny. More often than not, it's just uncomfortable. People come to comedy shows to laugh, not to be laughed at. As the one on stage with a microphone, you have all the power. To make fun of polite audience members without allowing them the means to respond is just taking advantage of your position. Nobody likes being laughed at, regardless or not of whether they've come to the show wearing a funny hat.

Note: The only exception to this rule is if you are being heckled. Being heckled is when somebody in the audience, who is unhappy with their life, becomes jealous of the fact that you're on stage getting all the attention, and they're stuck sitting in the dark listening to you. So, they decide to shout things out at you during your performance. If this happens to you, don't worry too much. It happens to all of us. And I'm not going to tell you what the correct way of dealing with it is, because, again, there isn't one. You just have to work out what you can do to get the focus back on your act, so you can finish it and leave the stage. If that means calling that person out and poking polite fun at them, then go for it. Me, I prefer to just ignore them. But to each his own. The only thing I will say though, is: if you are going to make fun of a heckler, don't be too aggressive. It will create an atmosphere in the room similar to the one that happens right after your parents have had a fight. Awkward and uncomfortable. Just make fun of them the way you'd make fun of your friends. Be biting, but not cruel. People will always like you more for it.

3. Be unoriginal

This one's also fairly self-explanatory. You're creating art, remember? Even if you don't realize it's art, it is. You are expressing yourself through your chosen medium, and if you're lucky, you're doing it in front of a willing audience. So think about it like that. Good art says something nobody has said before. Or it says it in a **way** nobody has said it before. That's your responsibility as the artist. Be original, be unique, say something that hasn't been said before. If you do, we'll remember you. Bad stand-up has a way of covering the same old subjects over and over again. "Women always want to *talk,* and men want to watch sports." I bet you've heard some variation on that idea before. Aside from just not being true, it's been done to death. Maybe it was funny the first time somebody thought of it and said it on stage, but that day is long gone now. It's like the famous stand-up cliché: "airline food."

In the 1980's, so many people did jokes about how bad airline food was, that it became a joke in it and of itself. To mention airline food on stage at a stand-up show is almost to make a joke about stand-up itself. It's done with the knowledge that everybody has done it before. It's the cliché to end all clichés. That's why, it's so important for you guys to be original. Whether that means talking about things that nobody has talked about before (which is hard), or talking about them with your own unique perspective (hard but not impossible), it will always benefit you to have a unique voice in your stand-up. Because people want to hear you talk about ideas that are as unique as you are.

Note: Does this mean you can't do jokes about airline food? No. You can totally make fun of airline food. But don't expect it to be easy. You're going to need to find a perspective on airline food that nobody has ever had before. If you can do that, I'll be impressed. Maybe I'll even send you a dollar in the mail.*

*I'm definitely not sending you a dollar in the mail.

Brain Worms Exercise

Late night setups

So, Late Night jokes are great. You may also know them as Monologue Jokes. They're called that because they're the sort of jokes the host tells at the beginning of a late night show like The Late Show With David Letterman, or Late Night with Jimmy Fallon. You've probably seen them if you ever stay up late and watch TV. The trick to writing them is to understand the simplicity of their format. It's two lines. That's it. Setup. Punchline. And you're done. The setup (the first line of the joke) is just something ripped from the headlines. The punchline (the second line) is where the funny comes in. And that's your job. I've done the first one for you. Now, you fill in the rest.

e.g.

1. Setup: "This week, the 3rd annual Clown Convention was held in Mexico City."

PL: "According to organizers, the convention is expected to start out funny, and then get extremely sad."

2. Setup: "This week, scientists discovered that chimpanzees perform better in memory tests than humans."

PL: "

_____

_____ "

3. Setup: "This week, researchers found that people who believe themselves to be ugly actually suffer from a brain   disorder that affects the way they see."

PL: "

_____

_____ "

4. Setup: "This week, the first car with a built-in robot was unveiled in Japan, and set for release in 2015."

PL: "

_____

_____ "

Chapter 5

DO'S

Okay, so now that we've covered all the negative things that you shouldn't do if you want to be a smart, original, awesome stand-up comic (and all around swell person), let's switch gears and talk about some things that you should do. Again, these aren't hard and fast rules - just helpful suggestions. Ignore them if you want, I won't hate you for it. You're your own person and blah blah blah. (Just don't expect me to come to your birthday party.)

1. Make friends with funny people

This is important. Why? Because it's really easy to get complacent, and to start thinking that because you make your friends laugh, you're the funniest person alive. Which is a really effective way of getting really lazy really quickly. And maybe you are the funniest person alive. But that doesn't mean you should rest on your laurels.

Luckily, one of the easiest ways to keep your joke-writing muscle toned and limber (gross image, I know) is to hang out with other funny people. If there's somebody at your school that you think is really funny or clever, try making friends with them. They're probably cool. Also, with the general standard of funniness raised, you'll find you have to work harder to stay on top of your game and to keep people laughing.

Healthy competition is exactly that - healthy. Also, as many of you no doubt have experienced already, being the only person in your group of friends who makes people laugh means you spend a lot of time working and almost no time laughing. So, try and switch it up a bit. I can tell you from experience that I never laugh more than when I'm hanging out and being goofy with a group of stand-up comic friends whom I respect and admire. Also, the moment when you manage to crack them up, and realize that you can hold your own among some seriously funny individuals: Priceless.

2. Collaborate

So, this is what you do after you've found some funny friends. Stand-up comedy is really lonely. Well, most of the time anyway. I mean, after a while you start to make friends with other stand-up comics at shows, and then you start seeing each other around and it becomes a bit less lonely, but when you're starting out, it's not exactly a cocktail party. Also, you'll spend a lot of your time on your own, writing jokes on your laptop, or working on material in your bedroom. So, how do you make it less lonely? Easy: you get a dog. Also, you start to collaborate with your funniest, most talented friends.

The best part of having talented friends is that you can use them. No, seriously. You can learn from them, and they from you. Everybody has a slightly different sense of humor, and every so often, when two complimentary senses of humor get together, magic happens. That's what you're looking for. So, start making YouTube videos with friends, write comic strips, start a satirical newspaper, review movies, write funny songs, record a podcast, write sketches, write scripts, hell, even do a 2-man routine if you want to. (There's a lot of really funny examples of those out there if you do some Googling.)

The point is, get our of your bedroom every now and then and collaborate with your funniest friends. Who knows, maybe you'll be the next comedy power duo? At the very least, you can eat pizza together and play video games, and that ain't half bad.

3. Be your own producer

So, now that you've made some funny friends, collaborated with a couple of them, and you're getting better as a comic, what next? Well, you could wait for Comedy Central to come to your house, knock on your door, and offer you your own prime-time television show, or...you could start taking control of your own comedy career. Nobody makes it overnight. Hell, most people never make it ever. But, that doesn't mean that you won't. If you work hard, and you're funny, and you're smart, and you're original, and you make your own opportunities, you have a great chance at making it somewhere, somehow.

But how do you get started? How do you get onto shows? How do you get stage time? All good questions. And there are a lot of different opinions on all of them. In my experience, the best way to get started doing shows, is to start your own. Don't wait for people to book you, start a show and book yourself. Find a coffee shop in your neighborhood, or an empty classroom at your school, or a talent show at your local mall, and start something. Not a fight, obviously. A comedy show. And maybe do it once a week, or once a month, or once a year. Whatever you want. And even if nobody shows up, or nobody listens, or everybody is too busy watching American Idol to listen to your intelligent musings on popular culture, at least you're putting yourself out there and getting stage time. It's absolutely the only way to get better.

Also, if the idea of starting your own show is a terrifying one, then start one with a friend. Or put up a flyer at your school asking if anybody is interested in co-hosting a show with you. Who knows, maybe there's somebody just like you out there and you didn't even know it.

4. Focus on getting better, not on getting famous

Everybody who expends the time and effort it takes to write and perform stand-up hopes to one day see their name in lights. Why? Because that means you've made it. Imagine what it must feel like to pack out a theater, or perform your stand-up on television, or have your own Comedy Central special. Pretty amazing, right? Right. Even right now as I write this, a lot of my friends are getting to realize those dreams, and I couldn't be prouder of them. What you're probably wondering though is how they got there. And the answer is: hard work. I know that sounds like a cliché, but it's actually true. The comics you see on television, and hear on the radio, and see on stage in front of thousands of people, made a decision a long time ago to be the best comics they could be. That means working hard, failing a lot, and always striving to be better. And bigger shows, packed-out theaters, and television spots are the rewards of that hard work. And it takes years. YEARS. And you've got to set your whole life towards earning it.

It's for that reason that it's important to set appropriate goals for yourself. Don't spend time worrying about how to get your Comedy Central special that you could be spending working on your jokes. I'm a firm believer in the idea that if you work hard at something, and you're nice to people, and you take pride in your work, then success will find you one way or another. A big pitfall for young comics (myself included) is thinking you're ready before you actually are. I remember doing my first stand-up show at a comedy club, and getting laughs, and thinking: Wow, I'm so good at this! The truth was that I had a good show. One good show. And looking back on it years later, I realize that the jokes were pretty terrible. Obvious, underdeveloped, and unoriginal. But how was I to know? I was too busy being focused on how to be a famous stand-up comic to worry about my material.

Anyway, as the story goes, I got cocky and by the time the next show rolled around, I thought I was pretty untouchable. I didn't work on my material at all, because I thought it was perfect. I might even have entertained the idea that somebody was going to see me, and then ask me to do stand-up on television. I was on my way to being a famous stand-up comic!

And then I bombed. Miserably. And I felt like an idiot. And it seriously sucked, and I hated my material, and the audience, and felt like quitting stand-up altogether. But I didn't quit, and now, looking back on it, I'm glad I did bomb. If I hadn't, I might never have been motivated to get better. So, learn from my mistake, and take things slow. Focus on getting better instead of getting famous, and maybe, one day, both will happen.

5. Challenge Yourself

This is maybe the most important one to remember. Because without it, you won't ever get any better. Have you ever been in one of those situations where you're nervous about doing something you've never done before, and then once you work up the courage to try it, you realize you're actually really good at it? Those situations are the best. I had that realization about giving speeches. Not to say that I'm like an amazing public speaker, but I was a really shy kid/teenager, and the idea of speaking in front of people used to terrify me. Then, in high school and college, I was forced to do it for various classes, and it actually ended up being really fun. And people enjoyed listening to me speak. And that was an amazing feeling. Thinking about it now, it's probably why I started doing stand-up after college. I love to talk.

Anyway, the point hidden in here somewhere is that challenging yourself is the only way to realize your potential as a writer and a performer. Avoid resting on your laurels, or doing the same jokes for the rest of your life. Push yourself to write about things that you don't think are inherently funny. Like being broken up with, or losing a loved one, or getting sick, or being sad. Some things may end up proving too difficult for you to make funny, but even just the attempt will serve you as a comic. You will train that joke-writing muscle in your brain to consider everything as potential material. And when it works? It's amazing.

There's a British comic I once saw in Edinburgh, who wrote and performed an entire 90-minute stand-up show all about the death of his aunt. It was equal parts moving and hilarious, and it was possibly the most impressive piece of stand-up I've ever seen. Why? Because it wasn't easy. Far from it. Can you imagine making the death of a loved one not only relatable to a room full of strangers, but funny too? That is a steep task. And not for the faint of heart. But he did it. And he came out of it with an amazing hour of stand-up comedy that not only made an audience laugh, it made them feel. And that's what it's all about.

Brain Worms Exercise

Worst _____

You know what's the worst? I don't know! So many things! And working it out will only help you with writing stand-up! So, get your brain into gear, and fill out this list with your own personal WORSTS.

What is the worst...

Movie you ever saw with your parents _____

_____

Gift you ever received

_____

Name for a dog you ever heard

_____

Book you ever read

_____

Food your mother ever cooked

_____

Nickname you ever got

_____

Item of clothing you ever owned

_____

Chapter 6

ADVICE FROM PEOPLE WHO AREN'T ME

So, I've given you a lot of advice so far. And you're probably tired of listening to me talk, in whatever voice you imagine (for the record, I'm a tenor. The sort of voice that would make a lot of money reading books on tape). And there's not a lot left to tell you. The thing about stand-up is, at a certain point, you sort of need to do all the work. I can give you pointers, and push you in the right direction, but ultimately it all comes down to you. Unless you write some of your own original stand-up, and unless you go somewhere and perform it in front of people, there's nothing more that I or anybody else can do to help you. So, go do that. It'll be scary, but, man, will it be worth it. Even if it totally sucks, which a lot of first times do, you'll still have had the guts to get up on stage and share your own unique perspective in front of a room full of people. That's pretty nuts.

So, there's not a lot more that I can tell you. But what about some other people? Maybe some other young people, just like you, who felt the same initial urge to get up on stage and say something? I asked a few of the young people in our program, some who have been writing and performing their own stand-up since they were old enough to hold a microphone (some of whom still wore diapers), to think of some advice they would give other young people, like yourself, who want to get into stand-up.

Finding good advice that actually helps you is like a finding a good movie to watch on television when you're flicking through channels at 1 in the morning over Christmas break: extremely rare, extremely satisfying, and hidden under a pile of missile-shooting helicopter chases. The point is, there's a lot of bad advice out there from people who have no business dishing it out. Be wary of it. It can lead you down the wrong path - a path paved with 'yo momma' jokes, observations about how much women love shopping, and terrible lispy impressions of gay people. That said, here's some good comedy advice from some teenaged comedy veterans.

Leo Frampton

"About six years ago, I told my mom, "I like to make people laugh, and I like it when people listen to me, can I do standup comedy?"

Who doesn't like people to listen to them? Boring people, I guess. Or people with nothing to say. Needless to say, you're probably somebody with something to say. Or hopefully, lots of somethings. Can you do stand-up comedy? The answer is the same as it was for Leo six years ago:

Who knows! But there's only one way to find out...

Leo goes on to say:

"There aren't many places in the world where someone with something good to say can put on a decent show. If you are a human being, which you probably are, chances are you have something to say that no one else does, and that certain something can definitely be funny. All it takes is finding that voice, and getting up on stage.

The more you explore your ideas and test them out on crowds, the better you'll get. When you make someone laugh, you are breaking past every emotional barrier there is, all their stress and judgment fades away for a moment of enjoyment. To generate a wave of laughter, to command the attention of a crowd, is one of the most satisfying and fulfilling experiences anyone can ever have, even if it takes pain and practice to get to that point. Anyone with interest in stand-up should work to get there, I promise it's possible."

See? Leo believes in you. And he doesn't even know you yet.

Charlie Bardey

"Don't be afraid of failure; sometimes, a joke just won't work, in which case, don't feel bad, move on, and silently curse the audience using gypsy magic."

Charlie is what we call a smart ass. That being said, he's funny, so that makes it more tolerable. And his point is one worth remembering. Audiences are as colorful and varied as a box of those magical jelly beans in Harry Potter. Sometimes, you'll luck out, and you'll get a warm and supportive crowd who really appreciates what you have to say. Other times, you'll get that one that tastes like boogers. You don't have much control over who comes through the doors, so you just have to do your best, and trust in your material. Do the jokes that you love to do.

Charlie adds:

"Observations don't always count as observational humor."

This is a great point. It's not enough to just notice something. You have to notice it and come to a conclusion. If you get up on stage and say "Snuggies are weird, aren't they?", you're only doing half the work. If they're weird, work out why and tell us in your own unique (and hopefully humorous) way.

Conor Williams

"Stand-up comedy is definitely an experience. You'll have good shows and bad shows, but you learn something new from each one. Every comedian is unique, and every time you get up on stage, you're being given a chance to characterize yourself and your personality through your jokes."

Absolutely. This is your chance to show us who you are. Don't waste it, yo!

"The most important part of comedy is being able to make fun of yourself. To me, comedy is never funny if it's making fun of others."

Another great point. Making fun of other people because it's easy is classic middle-school bully behavior. Never forget that the hardest person to lampoon is yourself. Try it whenever possible. It will only make you better.

Zach Rosenfeld

"To any future-comedians out there I would say, just do what you're happy with. You may not have the funniest life, but as long as you do what you love, and you do your best, and you're not afraid of making a fool out of yourself, that's comedy. "

True that. You don't need to have the craziest story in the world. Or the weirdest family. Or the most amazing life. You just need to have your own unique perspective on it, and work hard to find the funny in it.

David Thompson

"It's gotten to the point where I've immersed myself into such a deep level of sarcasm that it's difficult to actually be sincere. Which is hilarious and depressing."

God, me too. Get used to that. Thankfully we can hang out with other comedians.

"You just have to be yourself. You might see comedians on TV telling jokes about their jobs or their wives. You probably don't have a job yet, and hopefully you don't have a wife. Tell jokes that are about you. Anyone can make quips about airline food, but only you can tell us about the time your Uncle Sal had an allergic reaction on the plane inbound to your cousin's wedding.

Couldn't have said it better myself.

Lee Wolfowitz

"Stand-up comedy is a life raft in the middle of an ocean. I joined when I was drowning in the sea of adolescent cruelty and with the help of stand-up comedy, I was airlifted to the helicopter of being self fulfilled."

Lee is also a smart ass, but we love him for it. He's being facetious, but he actually makes a good point. Nobody gets into stand-up comedy because their lives are perfect. It's a form of expression that attracts complicated people who know what pain feels like. That pain can be losing at scrabble, or getting broken up with, or getting bad grades, or getting picked on, or being a child of divorce, or whatever. It doesn't matter. The point is, stand-up can help. I promise.

Luke Bergamini

"Stand-up comedy is like a traveling circus. Always interesting, and everybody involved with it is really weird."

Yep. And that's why we love it.

Brain Worms Exercise

Research assignment

A good stand-up comic can write jokes about pretty much anything. And with the internet being as awesome as it is, it's easy to research pretty much any topic you can imagine. So, with that in mind, try using Wikipedia or your local library to find out as much information as you can on the following topics, and see which facts you can use to turn into jokes. Who knows! You might end up writing a whole new routine!

Topics:

Hysteria

The Bubonic Plague

The Salem Witch Trials

Vampire Bats

The Crusades

Killer Bees

Stockholm Syndrome

The Heimlich Maneuver

Porphyria

Waterloo Teeth

The Ouija Board

WRITTEN BY:

David Smithyman

Failing to ever fulfill his true potential as an Australian child actor, David Smithyman moved to New York City in 2004 to try his hands at stand-up comedy. Whilst at NYU, he studied joke writing under staff writers from Seinfeld, The Simpsons and Late Night With Conan 'O Brien. Emerging from NYU with a degree in Television Writing and an award in comedy writing, David began regularly performing at clubs and bars around the city, until his control issues kicked in, and he began hosting his own comedy show in the Lower East Side (now in it's third year) and his own comedy trivia night in Brooklyn. He was also an extremely difficult teenager, which helps in his current line of work as the head teacher and producer at Kids 'N Comedy, where he spends his time arguing about video games, and helping teenaged comics realize their potential.

CONCEIVED BY: Karen Bergreen and Jo Ann Grossman

Karen Bergreen

Karen Bergreen has been teaching comedy to kids and adults for over ten years. She has appeared on Comedy Central's Premium Blend, New Joke City and Tough Crowd with Colin Quinn. In addition, Karen has appeared in the US Comedy Arts Festival, The Marshall's Women in Comedy Festival and at the Kennedy Center, and she performs regularly at all the major New York City clubs. Karen is the author of two comic mystery novels, Following Polly (an Oprah Magazine pick!) and Perfect is Overrated.

Jo Ann Grossman

Jo Ann Grossman is the co-founder of Kids 'N Comedy, formed in 1996. Jo Ann designed handmade sweaters for over 10 years sold in galleries and shops across the country and wrote "Modern Crochet for the Home" published by Ballantine. She was the associate editor for Parentage, a newsletter for parents over the age of 35, of which she was one. She and her husband, co-founder, Stu Morden, have one daughter, Emily Morden. Jo Ann is the producer and director of Kids 'N Comedy.

About Kids 'N Comedy

Kids 'N Comedy at the Gotham Comedy Club is the only place for kids age 10-18 to learn to write and perform their own original stand-up comedy. We provide a nurturing comedy community, and a space where teenagers can be themselves in all their smart, weird, edgy, baffling, adolescent glory. Our staff is made of a group of New York writers and comedians who, as teens, would have greatly benefitted from this program (and probably saved a lot of $$ on therapy.) Kids 'N Comedy has year round Saturday classes and summer camp. Visit us at www.kidsncomedy.com and say hello to us on Facebook. We're bored, and lonely, so we're bound to write you back.

Photo Credits;

Page 6: Conor Williams, Dillon Heverin, Emma Gonzalez and David Smithyman and Alejandro Kolleeny

Page 24 : (clockwise from the left corner) Zach Rosenfeld, Val Bodurtha, Charlie Bardey and Rachel Kaly

Page 40: : (clockwise from the left corner), Joe O'Hare, Marie McHugh, Luke Bergamini and Ryan Drum

Page 48: : (clockwise from the left corner) Lee Wolfowitz, Leo Frampton, Eric Kurn and Conor Carroll.

Page 57: : (clockwise from top), Camp Kids 'N Comedy 2009, David Thompson and Mark Cohen

Photo of Leo Frampton by Lee Wexler

Photo of Mark Cohen by Jonathan Slaff

All other photos by Jo Ann Grossman

Layout by: Ryan Fishman